OPRAH
WINFREY

THE ACHIEVERS

OPRAH
WINFREY

MEDIA SUCCESS STORY

Anne Saidman

 Lerner Publications Company ▪ Minneapolis

This book is available in two editions:
Library binding by Lerner Publications Company
Soft cover by First Avenue Editions
241 First Avenue North
Minneapolis, MN 55401

To my husband, Phil

LIBRARY OF CONGRESS CATALOGING-IN-PUBLICATION DATA

Saidman, Anne.
 Oprah Winfrey : media success story / Anne Saidman.
  p. cm.—(The Achievers)
 Summary: Examines the life of the actress and talk show host, from
her childhood on a farm in Mississippi to her achievements in
broadcasting and film.
 ISBN 0-8225-0538-X (lib. bdg.)
 ISBN 0-8225-9646-X (pbk.)
 1. Winfrey, Oprah—Juvenile literature. 2. Television
personalities—United States—Biography—Juvenile literature.
3. Motion picture actors and actresses—United States—Biography—
Juvenile literature. [1. Winfrey, Oprah. 2. Television
personalities. 3. Actors and actresses. 4. Afro-Americans—
Biography.] I. Title II. Series.
PN1992.4.W56S25 1990
791.45'092—dc20
[B]   90-38059
                   CIP
                   AC

Manufactured in the United States of America

International Standard Book Number: 0-8225-0538-X (lib. bdg.)
International Standard Book Number: 0-8225-9646-X (pbk.)
Library of Congress Catalog Card Number: 90-38059

3 4 5 6 7 8 9 10 99 98 97 96 95 94 93

Contents

Oprah liked to give speeches even as a child.

1

Head of the Class

Oprah stared out the window as she chewed her pencil. The five-year-old girl was writing a letter to her kindergarten teacher because she thought she belonged in a more advanced class. Most five-year-old children wouldn't be able to write a letter like that, but Oprah was unusual. She had learned how to read when she was only two and a half.

It was Oprah's grandmother, Hattie Mae Lee, who had taught her to read at such a young age. Oprah's parents were never married. When she was born, on January 29, 1954, her father, Vernon Winfrey, was away in the Army. Her mother, Vernita Lee, went to Milwaukee, Wisconsin, to work as a cleaning lady, and Oprah was left with Hattie Mae on a farm in Mississippi.

Hattie Mae was very strict with Oprah and beat her

whenever she misbehaved. But she also took care of Oprah and made all of her clothes. She taught Oprah to speak so well that her granddaughter was making Christmas and Easter speeches in church by the time she was three years old. Oprah's main duty on the farm was drawing water from the well and bringing it to the house. She also took the cows to pasture and fed the hogs.

Oprah was lonely on the farm. She didn't have any friends her own age until she went to school. She only saw television once or twice a year, when she went visiting with her grandmother on holidays. She says about that time of her life, "There weren't other kids, no playmates, no toys, except for one corncob doll. I played with the animals and talked to the cows."

Since Oprah was reading and making speeches when she was very young, it's not surprising that she didn't think she belonged in kindergarten. The teacher agreed with her, and she was moved into the first grade. Later she also skipped second grade.

When Oprah was six years old, Vernita, who by then had another child, arranged for Oprah to come live in Milwaukee. The three of them shared one room in a house owned by one of Vernita's friends. Meanwhile, Oprah's father, Vernon, had left the Army and was living in Nashville, Tennessee. He had two jobs, working as a janitor at Vanderbilt University and as a dishwasher at City Hospital. He and his wife Zelma didn't have any children, so he asked Vernita if Oprah could live in Nashville with them. Vernita was having a hard time being a single mother with two children, so she said yes.

Oprah moved in with her father and Zelma during the summer before she went into third grade. When school started, Zelma and Vernon required that Oprah read a book every week and write a report about it, and they made sure she added new words to her vocabulary every week. For the first time in her life, Oprah was outgoing and popular. Also, since Zelma and Vernon were active church members, religion became very important to Oprah.

At the same time, back in Milwaukee, Vernita was sorry she had let Oprah go to live with Vernon and Zelma. Vernita didn't want to take Oprah out of school in the middle of the school year, though. She waited until Oprah visited her the next summer. By then, Vernita had a third child. She told Oprah she was planning to get married and pressured Oprah to stay in Milwaukee. Oprah agreed. Vernon wasn't happy with this arrangement, but he did not feel he could do anything to change it.

Vernita Lee's promised marriage never happened. Oprah continued to get good grades at her new school in Milwaukee, but she wasn't popular as she had been in Nashville. The other students called her "the bookworm." Looking back on her unhappy school years, Oprah says: "I believe in trying to be the best because that's what has always worked for me. If you grow up a bully and that works, that's what you do. I was always the smartest kid in class and that worked for me—by third grade I had it figured out. So I was the one who would read the assignment early and turned in the paper ahead of time. That makes everyone else hate you, but that's what worked for me."

Being unpopular wasn't Oprah's only problem. When she was nine years old, a male cousin raped her. Some of Vernita's friends sexually abused Oprah as well. Oprah believed that somehow she was responsible for the abuse. She never told anyone about it until many years later, during an emotional moment on her television show. She says, "I didn't tell anybody about it because I thought I would be blamed for it. I remember blaming myself for it, thinking something must be wrong with me."

Once when Oprah visited her father in Nashville, she made a speech at a church and was paid $500. The experience made her realize what she wanted to do with her life. She came home from the church and told her father that she planned to be famous and that she wanted to get paid to talk when she grew up.

2

Growing Up

When Oprah was 13, she entered Lincoln High School. One of Oprah's teachers realized how smart she was and arranged for her to receive a full scholarship to Nicolet High School. Nicolet was a private school in a rich suburb of Milwaukee. It was 1968, and a few bright black students were being sent to Nicolet as an experiment in integration.

Oprah was very popular at Nicolet, and something of a curiosity as well. Mothers of other students encouraged their children to invite Oprah to come home with them after school. For white students, it was "in" at the time to know someone who was black.

Oprah soon felt pressured to keep up with her new, rich friends. Vernita didn't have any extra money to give Oprah so that she could do things with her classmates, like going out for pizza after school. Oprah began to steal money from Vernita's purse.

Around this time Oprah also began to feel that she was not good-looking. She hated her eyeglasses, but Vernita said she couldn't afford to buy another pair. Oprah tore apart their apartment and broke her eyeglasses. She told the police there had been a robbery and pretended that she didn't remember anything.

Oprah's plan was both a success and a failure. When Vernita heard that the "robbers" had broken the eyeglasses, she realized that the culprit was Oprah. Nevertheless, she still had to buy Oprah another pair — which was, of course, exactly what Oprah had wanted in the first place.

Oprah continued to misbehave and even ran away several times. Finally Vernita realized that she couldn't handle her daughter, and she called Vernon. He brought Oprah back to Nashville to live with him and Zelma. "My father saved my life," Oprah says about the move. "I am what I am because of him."

Vernon and Zelma were very strict with Oprah. They made her change the way she dressed: no more halter tops, no more short, tight skirts, and much less makeup. Zelma took Oprah to the library every two weeks. Oprah had to choose five books, and before the next library visit she had to read them and write reports about them. Vernon and Zelma also limited Oprah's television viewing to one hour a day.

Oprah attended Nashville's East High School. She was one of the first blacks to integrate the school, just

Oprah poses with classmates at East High School.

Oprah was one of the first black students to attend East High.

as she had been one of the first blacks to integrate Nicolet High School in Milwaukee. The difference was that this time her classmates didn't have more money than she did. She got good grades and became more self-confident.

In 1970, when Oprah was 17, she was invited to attend the White House Conference on Youth in Estes Park, Colorado. She had been chosen to represent East High School as an outstanding U.S. teenager because of her academic achievements and her involvement in school activities. That year she also joined the high school drama club and won first place in a speech contest. Her involvement in school and extracurricular activities eventually led to her first radio job.

3

On the Air

During Oprah's senior year in high school, she participated in a March of Dimes Walkathon. Looking for people to sponsor her in the Walkathon, she went into the studios of WVOL, a Nashville radio station. One of the disc jockeys agreed to be a sponsor; he would give the March of Dimes a certain amount of money for each mile Oprah walked in the Walkathon.

A few weeks later, when she returned to collect the money from him, the disc jockey told her that he liked her speaking voice. In fact, he thought that she might be able to work in the radio business. He asked her to make a tape for him.

WVOL's station manager liked the tape and hired Oprah as a part-time worker. She started out doing newscasts on the weekend, and then she began working weekdays after school.

Oprah landed her first radio job while she was still in high school.

Shortly after Oprah began working at WVOL, the station manager asked Oprah to represent WVOL in Nashville's Miss Fire Prevention Contest. She entered the contest and won.

The summer after Oprah graduated from East High School, she worked part time for WVOL. In the fall she registered as a full-time student at Tennessee State University, majoring in speech and drama, and continued to work part time at WVOL. She took classes in the morning and worked in the afternoon.

Tennessee State University was an all-black college that was caught up in the civil rights movement at the time. Oprah felt alienated from the other students.

They were becoming activists, but she wasn't interested in politics and didn't participate in the protests for equal rights. Looking back on her college years, Oprah says, "I felt that most of the kids hated and resented me. They were into black power and anger. I was not."

In March 1972, Oprah won the Miss Black Nashville Pageant at the Nashville Elks Club. As a result, Oprah represented Nashville in the first Miss Black Tennessee Pageant in June. She won that pageant as well—to her surprise, because she didn't consider herself very attractive. Her prizes were a college scholarship and a trip to Hollywood for the Miss Black America Pageant.

At the Miss Black America Pageant, Oprah insisted on competing only on the basis of her personality and poise. She refused to showcase her looks. During the pageant she acted composed and confident. She didn't win, but people who were there said afterward that she didn't seem disappointed at all.

In September 1973, Oprah was asked to audition for a news position at WTVF-TV in Nashville. The television station wanted someone who would be authoritative but friendly, like a next-door neighbor who could tell you what was going on.

Although Oprah was nervous at the audition, she didn't let it show, and she was hired. She became the first female co-anchor and the first black co-anchor in Nashville. She knew she was being hired partly because the station had to fill a quota for a certain number of minority employees, but she said, "Sure I was a token. But honey, I was one happy token."

At WTVF-TV, Oprah worked on the weekend news and wrote her own scripts. Sometimes she also worked as a reporter, which was difficult for her. She always got emotionally involved with the story and cared too much about the people she was interviewing.

After a while, Oprah stopped attending Tennessee State University because working at WTVF-TV was a full-time job. She didn't actually receive her degree in speech and performing arts until much later.

Soon Oprah was promoted from co-anchoring the weekend news to co-anchoring the weeknight news. In 1976 she left WTVF-TV to become a co-anchor and a reporter at WJZ-TV in Baltimore, Maryland. She had good reasons for making the move. Not only did the job pay more than she was making, but it would give her a chance to be on her own instead of living with Vernon and Zelma. She was also being offered a more prominent position in a larger market, which meant that more people would be watching her.

4

Moving Forward

Oprah moved to Baltimore in June 1976. To advertise her arrival, WJZ-TV plastered billboards all over the city. The billboards read: "What's an Oprah?" Oprah's news show premiered on August 16, 1976. She was stiff and uncomfortable, and it didn't work out. She was a good co-anchor but not a good reporter. She never did learn how to keep from getting involved with her subjects. Once she tried to refuse to cover a particularly upsetting story and was told she'd be fired. She reported the story and apologized to the television audience.

In April of 1977 Oprah was removed from the evening anchor slot and given other assignments. She would be doing early morning inserts on the "Good Morning America" show and working with WJZ-TV's Instant Eye Unit as a reporter.

She felt that she was being demoted, but things got even worse. WJZ-TV's assistant news director decided that Oprah's image had to change. Oprah was sent to a speech coach to change her speaking style and to a fancy beauty parlor for a permanent, which made all of her hair fall out. She was left totally bald.

Oprah felt awful. She couldn't find any wigs to wear while her hair was growing back, because her head was too large. She said about that period of her life, "There's not a wig made to fit my head . . . so I had to walk around wearing scarves. All my self-esteem was gone. My whole self-image. I cried constantly."

As if things weren't hard enough for Oprah, as part of her assignment to work with WJZ-TV's Instant Eye Unit, she was being sent out to cover tragedies. According to Oprah, "I really wasn't cut out for the news. I'd have to fight back the tears if a story was too sad. I just didn't have the detachment." She was under tremendous pressure. She turned to food for comfort and gained a lot of weight.

Later that spring, a new station manager arrived at WJZ-TV and began to make changes. The new manager wanted to launch a morning talk show that could compete with the popular "Phil Donahue Show." The manager called the new program "People Are Talking," and he picked Oprah to co-host it.

Oprah thought this was the new station manager's way of easing her out of the news—and then out of

The management at WJZ-TV wanted to change Oprah's image, but the results were disastrous. Luckily, her hair grew back.

the station. But she changed her mind, because she realized very quickly that talk shows were what she did best. "Talk shows have liberated me," she says. "They put me on the talk show just to get rid of me, but it was really my saving grace. The first day I did it, I thought, 'This is what I really should have been doing all along.'"

Oprah was thrilled with "People Are Talking," but other parts of her life weren't going so well. When her boyfriend, Lloyd Kramer, moved to New York, Oprah coped with her loneliness by overeating. She also took on extra assignments at WJZ-TV to keep herself busy and ended up with no time for a social life. Debbie DiMaio, the producer of "People Are Talking," said she had never seen anyone work as hard as Oprah.

Oprah co-hosted "People Are Talking" for seven years. Eventually she began to feel restless. As her self-confidence grew, she realized that she wanted to host a show by herself instead of being a co-host. She was soon to get her chance.

Debbie DiMaio applied to WLS-TV in Chicago for a position as producer of the "A.M. Chicago" show. The show, which combined information and entertainment, also needed a host. When the WLS-TV executives saw Oprah on DiMaio's audition tape, they offered Oprah a job as the show's host. DiMaio also got the job as producer.

On September 4, 1983, Oprah went to Chicago and signed a four-year contract with WLS-TV. She was worried about making such a big move, and one way she handled her fears was by eating. She explained later, "Everybody kept telling me that it was going to be impossible to succeed because I was going into Phil Donahue's hometown. So you know, I'd eat and eat. I'd eat out of the nervousness of it all."

She started hosting "A.M. Chicago" in January of 1984, and it was an immediate success. The show received great ratings. Oprah convinced her bosses that she didn't need to use prepared scripts and cue cards. She was given a lot of freedom, and that made her more relaxed. To prepare for a show, at the end of each day she would be given a packet of information about the next day's program. She would read it and then decide what questions she wanted to ask the guests.

When Oprah first began hosting the "A.M. Chicago" show, Phil Donahue, a native of Chicago, had dominated the local talk-show scene for 16 seasons. Before long, Oprah's show was getting better ratings than Donahue's. Oprah said, "I like Phil Donahue, but I have to admit it, it feels good to beat him. For the longest time, I couldn't go about doing my job without people saying, 'Yeah, you're good. But are you as good as Donahue?'" Nevertheless, Oprah gives Phil Donahue credit for setting high standards for talk shows aimed at women.

Some of the famous people Oprah has interviewed on the show include Stevie Wonder, Billy Dee Williams, Christie Brinkley, Candice Bergen, Paul McCartney, Goldie Hawn, and Maya Angelou.

On February 10, 1993, in a prime-time television special, Oprah spoke with Michael Jackson in the first live interview he had given in 14 years. A notoriously

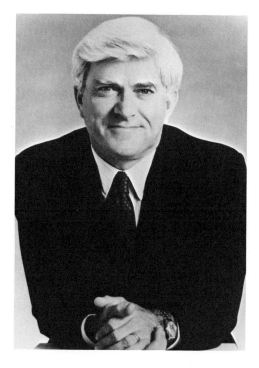

Oprah's main talk show rival was Phil Donahue.

private man, Michael Jackson usually refuses to be interviewed. Yet, he did not refuse Oprah. This milestone in the entertainment business emphasized Oprah's talent as an interviewer and as a businesswoman.

Oprah has also hosted many subject-oriented shows, about issues such as child abuse, agoraphobics (people who are afraid to leave their homes), blindness, the Ku Klux Klan, nudists, and satanic cults. People have made fun of some of the topics the show has covered, but that sort of criticism has never bothered Oprah. "I really think you can do anything with good taste," she insists.

At the end of Oprah's first year with "A.M. Chicago," *Newsweek* magazine published a full-page article about her. A member of Johnny Carson's "Tonight Show" staff read the article and invited Oprah to appear on the show.

In September 1985, as further proof of Oprah's success, the name of the show was changed from "A.M. Chicago" to the "Oprah Winfrey Show," and it was expanded from 30 minutes to an hour.

Oprah's popularity was soaring, but she still wished she had a boyfriend. She wasn't interested in casual dating, however; she didn't want to see anyone unless she thought he was special. Besides, she was very busy. Aside from her show, she had five to six speaking engagements every week. She especially enjoyed speaking to underprivileged teenagers, encouraging them to stay in school.

Because Oprah's own school experience focused on books, she still loved to read. One of the books Oprah read was Alice Walker's Pulitzer Prize-winning novel, *The Color Purple*, and it made a strong impression on her. She liked the book so much that she gave a copy of it to anyone and everyone. She gave the book to people getting married or divorced, having a baby, receiving a promotion at work, or throwing a housewarming. But even Oprah didn't know what a difference the book was going to make in her life.

Oprah played Sofia in *The Color Purple.*

5

From TV to the Movies

Quincy Jones, who was coproducing the film version of *The Color Purple*, flew to Chicago in 1985 to testify in a lawsuit. While he was there, he turned on the television set in his hotel room and saw Oprah on the screen. He knew immediately that she would be perfect for the part of Sofia, an important role in the movie.

Oprah was thrilled to be chosen for the role, but she was nervous about being the only actor in the film with no previous acting experience. Despite her self-doubts, she flew to North Carolina to film the movie. While she was gone, WLS-TV used guest hosts and ran repeats of Oprah's most popular shows.

Oprah felt that Sofia, the character she played in the movie, had a lot to teach people. Sofia's most important lesson was that no matter how much people

Film critics praised Oprah's performance as Sofia.

get beaten down, they can always find a way to pull themselves back together and heal. That attitude describes exactly the way Oprah feels about the problems her shows deal with and about the people who have suffered through those problems. Oprah believes that people who feel powerless, who are victims, can take control of their lives and change.

During the filming of the movie, when she wasn't busy, Oprah read a novel by Gloria Naylor called *The Women of Brewster Place*. It was another book that would become important to her.

When filming of *The Color Purple* was completed, Oprah was depressed. She felt that it was the best

Oprah takes a break on the set with Quincy Jones, coproducer of *The Color Purple.*

Oprah was disappointed that *The Color Purple* didn't win any
Academy Awards.

experience she had ever had, and nothing else would ever match it.

The Color Purple was nominated for 11 Academy Awards, including one for Oprah in the Best Supporting Actress category. Oprah set a goal for herself to lose weight by the night of the Oscar awards ceremony, but she wasn't able to achieve her goal. In her disappointment, she figured that she might as well eat and enjoy it. Instead of losing weight, she gained weight.

Oprah's inability to slim down wasn't the only frustration that she had to face. Oprah did not receive the award for Best Supporting Actress, and *The Color Purple* did not win a single award out of the 11 nominations. Oprah was disappointed and angry, but those feelings didn't stop her from wanting to act in more movies in the future. In the meantime, she concentrated on her talk show.

6

Spectacular Success

In 1986 the "Oprah Winfrey Show" began to be shown on television stations across the United States. The only change Oprah made was to leave out references to Chicago so that her show could be enjoyed by viewers all over the country. Otherwise she kept everything the same.

Oprah's first national show, which was broadcast on September 8, 1986, was about how to find love. The show was seen on television stations in 138 cities. Nearly all of the reviews were enthusiastic.

Also in 1986, Oprah's love life began to improve. She started dating Stedman Graham, a 6'6" former model and basketball player with a graduate degree in education. Stedman headed a program called Athletes Against Drugs, which counseled young people about the dangers of drug abuse.

Oprah and Stedman had already met, having run into each other at various Chicago social functions. Stedman kept asking Oprah out, but she always refused. She felt intimidated by his good looks. But one day when he called to ask her out, she was very tired—too tired to say no. She went out with him and decided that she wanted to see him again. Stedman had many qualities Oprah admired in a man: he was taller than she, he wasn't threatened by her success, and he had his own money.

It was also around this time that Oprah made another movie, *Native Son*, which was released in December 1986. *Native Son* did not receive good reviews, but many critics praised Oprah's performance.

In the summer of 1986, Oprah bought a luxurious condominium in a Chicago skyscraper. It sat on the 57th floor, with a panoramic view of the Chicago skyline and Lake Michigan. Her new apartment had a master bedroom suite, guest room, library, living room, dining room, kitchen, several bathrooms, sauna, laundry room, and even a crystal chandelier in the closet. She said she bought the apartment to celebrate the achievement of her goal to become a millionaire by the age of 32.

Oprah had come a long way and had gone through many changes in her life. She says, "I always knew something big was going to happen to me. I just knew." Luck played a part in her success, but she also made it happen: "Not a day goes by that I do not consciously

Oprah with Stedman Graham

say, 'Thank you. I'm truly blessed.' But I also believe that you tend to create your own blessings. You have to prepare yourself so that when opportunity comes, you're ready."

With her new success, Oprah wanted to give something back to her family. She bought her mother a condominium in Milwaukee, and she tried to help her father retire. But Vernon, a part-time city councillor as well as a full-time barber and the co-owner of a general store, refused. Much to Oprah's disappointment, the only things her father ever asked her for were tickets to the Mike Tyson-Michael Spinks fight, new tires for his truck, and a better television set for his barbershop so he could watch her show while he worked.

In May 1987, Oprah finally received her diploma from Tennessee State University. That year she sponsored 10 full scholarships at the university, totaling $750,000. She managed the scholarship fund herself, paying for everything the students needed: tuition, room and board, books, and spending money. She insisted that the students maintain good grades and threw them out of the program if they did not.

Despite all the possibilities her wealth presented, Oprah spent most of her time thinking about her show. By that time, it had a viewing audience of about 10 million people and appeared on 198 stations throughout the country.

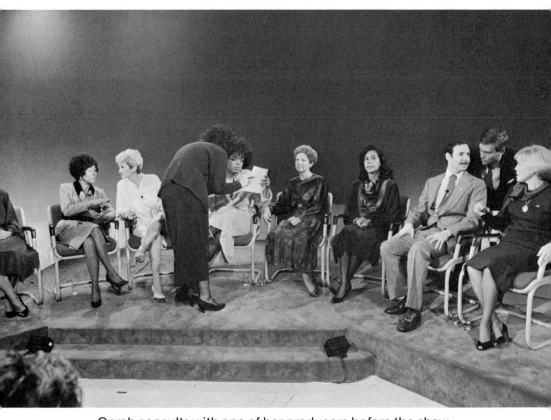

Oprah consults with one of her producers before the show.

Oprah's success is due to many things. She tries hard to bring many wonderful qualities to her show: folksy warmth, honesty, humor, spontaneity, enthusiasm, and a sassy spirit. She has a knack for getting people to reveal things on national television that they wouldn't have imagined telling anyone. She isn't afraid to discuss her own problems either, including her constant

Privacy is a thing of the past for Oprah.

battle to lose weight. And finally, she likes to end each show by personally saying good-bye to every member of the studio audience.

Oprah likes to employ women and minorities as her staff members, to try to combat the discrimination they often experience on the job market. Most of her employees regard her as a sister or adviser. Debbie DiMaio, the executive producer of the "Oprah Winfrey Show," says, "I feel very destined to have met her. I have pretty much unconditional love for her." Oprah is generous with the people on her staff, who have described her as demanding and fair. She is a perfectionist who expects excellence from both herself and her staff.

Oprah either walks or drives to work, depending on the weather. Often times she will work as long as 14 hours a day. Afterward, she likes to go out and relax, but it's hard to do because fans keep coming up to her. She complains, "You're never allowed to be private. You never, ever, ever have moments to yourself, and you're always conscious that people are looking at you."

When Oprah spends money on herself, it's usually on luxury items that she could not afford when she was younger. She likes to spend time personalizing her apartment, making it look especially "Oprah-like."

Oprah prays, reads her Bible often, and goes to church regularly. She also has a fondness for novels, history books, and biographies about black women.

Oprah and some of her staff members have formed a Big Sisters group with two dozen economically disadvantaged girls in a Chicago housing project. Oprah worked hard at the Big Sisters group, in part because she believed that she might have become an unwed teenage mother herself if she hadn't gone to live with her father. She said of her work there, "We tell the kids, if you want affection you don't need a baby. Get a kitten!"

Her goal was to encourage the girls in the group to stay in school, get an education, and take responsibility for their futures. Her advice to them has a lot to do with how she sees herself: "I don't think of myself as a poor deprived ghetto girl who made good. I think of myself as somebody who from an early age, knew I was responsible for myself, and I had to make good."

7

Oprah and Harpo

In 1988 Oprah was named "Broadcaster of the Year" by the radio and television industry. In November of the same year, Oprah gained full ownership of her talk show. In exchange for ownership, she agreed to continue the talk show for at least five more years. Owning her show means that Oprah has full control over it. She can schedule the show's production in ways that give her the time she needs for other television and movie projects.

Oprah made two major purchases in 1988. She bought a 160-acre farm in Indiana, where she often spends weekends with Stedman. She also bought a production studio in Chicago, becoming the first black woman to own her own television and film complex. She named the studio Harpo, which is "Oprah" spelled backwards.

Gloria Steinem introduced Oprah as *Ms.* magazine's Woman of the Year in 1989.

Oprah had high hopes for Harpo Productions. She wanted to create a place so stimulating and comfortable that employees would love coming to work. She wanted the studio to attract new business to Chicago, creating new jobs and helping the economy. She also wanted Harpo to become a creative force in the entertainment industry, producing high-quality work. She said, "I want to do movies that are about something, that move people and leave them feeling uplifted."

Oprah spent $20 million to buy and renovate the studio. It fills an entire block in Chicago and is the largest film and television production studio in the Midwest. The studio was built to house Oprah's staff offices, a cafeteria, and an exercise room. From the start, Oprah has been an essential part of every Harpo project and has signed every check herself.

At one point, Oprah earned an estimated $30 million a year, which made her one of the wealthiest self-made women in the United States. She said that she found the money—and the power that went with it—humbling. With her increased success and income, her involvement with humanitarian work also increased. Her mission developed into educating people about the black experience.

The first Harpo production was a made-for-television movie of Gloria Naylor's novel, *The Women of Brewster Place*. The book follows the lives of seven black women living in a poor section of a large city. Oprah had a

big role in the movie, as Mattie, a wise woman who helps her neighbors. She was also the film's executive coproducer. To free up her time to film the movie, Oprah taped four weeks of her talk show in advance.

Once the filming actually began, Oprah found that in addition to acting, she had to make production decisions—like whether people working on the set should have to pay for their own breakfasts. Oprah tried not to abuse her authority. She worked hard and was the first person to arrive every morning. She said, "You can work 18 hours a day and still be pleasant. I made sure I knew everybody's name so there was no one thinking I was Miss Mightier-Than-Thou."

For Oprah, the filming of *The Women of Brewster Place* evoked memories of her troubled childhood. She said, "If you have lived as a black person in America, you know all of those women, you just know them. They're your aunts, your mother, your cousins, your nieces." When she had to feed chickens for a scene in the film, she said: "I have life experience of saying, 'Here, chick, chick, chick.' I used to do it on my grandmother's farm when I was four years old. It's very therapeutic and boring. It's great in a movie scene for five minutes, but not so great if you have to do it every day."

The Women of Brewster Place aired on television in

Opposite: Oprah starred in and produced the TV movie *The Women of Brewster Place.*

47

March 1989. The critics said that it was moving, despite some awkward sections. Some complained that the movie did not come close to achieving its potential and that black men were portrayed in a negative way.

Getting *The Women of Brewster Place* filmed was a major accomplishment for Oprah, but it wasn't her only success that year. She went on a medically supervised diet, and in 1988 she was finally able to lose weight. She hired a cook to prepare nutritious meals and snacks, and she did an hour of aerobic exercises every day. She lost a total of 67 pounds: "Right now I feel about as good as you can feel and still live." In the November 15 episode of her show, Oprah explained how she had lost the weight. Almost half of all Americans watched the show!

Oprah had her share of misfortune in 1989 as well: one of her half-brothers died of AIDS. Also, toward the end of 1989, Oprah admitted that she had gained back 17 of the 67 pounds she had lost, discovering "that the battle only begins with losing the weight and that keeping it off is really the true challenge." She thought she would be able to lose the weight she had regained. It was typical of Oprah to discuss her weight troubles on her show, in front of millions of viewers.

Despite her attempts to get and stay thin, since 1989 she has gained back all 67 of the pounds she so dramatically lost. She talked about her weight problem on one of her shows entitled "The Pain of Regain." She

The Women of Brewster Place became the basis for Oprah's TV series "Brewster Place."

claimed that most dieters regain the weight they lose because diets do not work. She talked about her pain and disappointment: "My greatest failure was in believing that the weight issue was just about weight. It's not. It's about being able to say no."

Oprah wants to like herself just as she is. She explains her new efforts: "Trying to live and not be controlled by food has been an ongoing process for me. It's a behavior I'm trying to learn." She is frustrated that her weight has received so much public attention. And although she assumes much of the responsibility for making it so public, she also declares, "I'm sick of it, sick, sick, sick, sick, sick, sick, sick." Rather than trying to lose weight and get thin, Oprah's new goals are "getting healthy, getting fit, and being strong."

On top of having a successful talk show, a career as a movie actress, and her own production company, Oprah recently opened a restaurant in Chicago called "Eccentric." The foods on the menu include some of Oprah's favorites, like mashed potatoes with horse-radish and chicken "pummeled and thwapped" and coated in Parmesan bread crumbs.

But one of Oprah's more important concerns is child abuse. She has publicly stated that she was sexually abused when she was nine years old. This abuse continued until she was 14 and moved to Nashville to live with her father. The sexual abuse and murder of a little girl from Chicago by a convicted child abuser in mid-February forced Oprah into action. She wanted to prevent child abuse from happening at all, and she wanted immediate action.

In February of 1991, Oprah hired a talented lawyer from a prominent Chicago law firm to help her draft a legislative bill and get it passed as a law. On November 12, Oprah presented her bill to the U.S. Senate Judiciary Committee. Her bill proposes the creation of

In 1989, Oprah opened Eccentric, a restaurant in Chicago.

a national data bank of information about convicted child abusers. This would prevent them from getting jobs working with children. With a few changes to her proposal, the committee accepted the bill and it is now awaiting action from the Senate.

After a disappointing and heart-wrenching year, 1992 brought excitement and happiness. On October 10, Stedman Graham proposed marriage, and a joyous, unbelieving Oprah accepted. They told only very close friends for a few weeks, but it soon became national news. They have not yet set a date but plan to be married in 1993. Although they have been dating for six years, she and Stedman didn't let the media pressure them into getting married before they were ready.

Once Oprah's favorite response to questions about her love life was, "Mr. Right's coming, but he's in Africa and he's *walkin'*." Although she was reluctant to go out with Stedman at first, she seems to have found the man of her dreams. Oprah describes Stedman as genuine, kind, and supportive: "Lots of people want to ride with you in the limo. But you want someone who'll help you catch the bus." Oprah is finally making room in her life for the family she has always wanted. She seems quite happy to make the adjustment.

As is her habit, Oprah keeps reaching higher and higher, demanding more and more from life. Who knows what she will try next? "When I look at the future," she has said, "it's so bright it burns my eyes."

ACKNOWLEDGMENTS

The photographs in this book are reproduced through the courtesy of: Hollywood Book and Poster, pp. 1, 21, 25, 28, 30, 31, 54; Photofest, pp. 2, 22, 46, 49; Bettman Newsphotos, pp. 6, 39, 44; East Middle School Library, pp. 13, 16; Cliff Lewis, p. 14; Paul Natkin/Starfile, p. 26; Kevin Mazur/London Features International, p. 34; Jorie Gracen/London Features International, p. 37; Robin Kaplan/London Features International, p. 40; Lettuce Entertain You Enterprises Inc., p. 51; Walter McBride/Retna Ltd., p. 52; Bob Brooks, p. 55. Front cover photograph by Kevin Mazur/London Features International. Back cover photograph courtesy of Bettman Newsphotos.

ABOUT THE AUTHOR

Besides being a school librarian and a writer, Anne Saidman is a photographer and a juggler. She lives in Brooklyn, New York, with her husband and their son.